KU-213-133

All Things Weird and Wonderful

For Flossie ~
all that courage, heart and love...

All Things Weird and Wonderful

Stewart Henderson

Illustrated by Nigel Baines

LION
Children's Books

644501   SCH
J 821.08

Text copyright © 2003 Stewart Henderson
Illustrations copyright © 2003 Nigel Baines
This edition copyright © 2003 Lion Publishing

The moral rights of the author and illustrator
have been asserted

Published by
Lion Publishing plc
Mayfield House, 256 Banbury Road,
Oxford OX2 7DH, England
www.lion-publishing.co.uk
ISBN 0 7459 4678 X

First edition 2003
1 3 5 7 9 10 8 6 4 2 0

All rights reserved

A catalogue record for this book is available
from the British Library

Typeset in 12/16 ITC Century Book
Printed and bound in Great Britain
by Biddles Ltd, Guildford and King's Lynn

Contents

Always making things

I made the splash,
the whirlpool, the surf,
the wonder of thunder,
the sounds of the earth.

I formed the egg,
the armpit, the pear,
the parrot, the carrot,
the goat's glassy stare.

I shaped the twig,
the walrus, the stoat,
the leopard, the shepherd,
the toad's puffing throat.

I breathed the bud,
the iris, the haze,
the tiger, the Eiger,
the ticking of days.

I thought the sprout,
the cactus, the deep,
the blossom, the possum,
the donkey asleep.

I grew the sap,
the desert, the dawn,
the eagle, the beagle,
the mown summer lawn.

I dreamt the wren,
Orion, the kiss,
the moose and the goose and
the cat's arch-backed hiss.

I made the ant,
the vastness, the dew –

But the best of my heart
and the height of my heart
and the light of my heart
was
when I made you.

Above us...

Space is ace

Space is ace
mysterious
above
beyond
around
the universe is singing
this huge, galactic sound
as Venus, Neptune, Jupiter
in three-part harmony
read stars as crochets, quavers,
arranged by Mercury.

Space is ace
astonishing
expanding
going on
to who knows where.
The later place?
The birth room of the sun?
Up there
are many guesses
of untamed territory,
a stellar census we can't count,
a wild tranquillity.

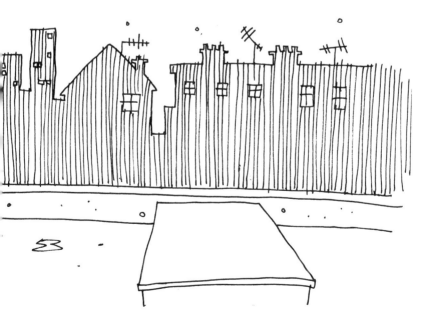

Moon message

New,
First Quarter,
Full,
Last Quarter,
torch,
reflective
flare,
in the twinkling ink
of winter
breathing
without
air.

Changing places

The day is disappearing,
she's off to meet the night
where she will share with darkness
the present that is light,

like sunrise, sparkling oceans,
the middle of July,
the oak tree and the blue jay,
the hopscotch butterfly.

The day is disappearing
as light begins to fade,
the night-time's tinsel treasures
are ready to parade:

the helicopter fireflies
and bats in cloak-like flight,
the comets, stars and planets,
the grotto of the night.

So let us praise the noon-shine
and celebrate the night.
The diamanté darkness
and the dancing light.

There are two bears on the moon

There are two bears on the moon
where they keep their honey jars
there are two bears on the moon
and both are made of stars

one's named Ursa Major
the bigger of the two
the other's Ursa Minor
he never really grew

you'll see them with a telescope
if you really try
their coats are constellations
in the Northern sky

but when they're done with shining
they amble down from space
and treat the lunar landscape
as their merrymaking place

they romp and roll down craters
then race off to their den
hibernate but not for long
then do it all again

there are two bears on the moon
don't bother asking how
there are two bears on the moon
and they're waving at you now

Old star looks back

(A newly identified star in the southern Milky Way may be the oldest ever found. It is estimated at between 14 and 15 billion years old.)

Have you ever seen a chariot race, live?
I have…
… or the planning drawings of the Pyramids
or a pharaoh in the bath
or a dodo
or three kings looking lost?
I even saw England win the World Cup
but that was such a long time ago.

Were you there during
the Ice Age,
the signing of the Magna Carta,
Bonnie Prince Charlie's skedaddle to Skye,
or the Hundred Years War,
which, in fact, was over in no time?

Do you know where to find
the trowel used on the Great Wall of China,
King Arthur's sword,
the very first wheel,
or the secret pastures of the buffalo?

Have you heard
a supernova explosion,
or the sound of exploratory space craft,
or black holes yawning?
I could go on
but I'd overwhelm you…
… but have you considered stars older
than me?
or a.........?
or......?
or...?

Through another day

I slouch and mumble through another day

realize I've forgotten my Maths homework
which I didn't actually do

dream up new excuses
for forgetting my Maths homework
without letting on that I haven't done it

get told off for texting in class

repeat 'I'm so bored'
as a motto and reason for everything

while meanwhile
in the astral amphitheatre

high above
this small square of earth

enormous giants
face each other

supergigantic stars called
Alpha and Beta

so big that we need
a new word for big

Alpha and Beta
red and blue opponents
with the energy output
of thousands upon thousands upon thousands
   of suns
like never-ending Maths
which I can't add up
and which I couldn't do anyway

and all fantastically meaningful

although I don't know what it means

they're above us
now
in the burning there

while I'm in this little here
offering a pathetic story
as to why I've forgotten my Maths homework
which I didn't do anyway.

You are such a different angel

You are such a different angel,
talons primed for arched attack,
sniper's eye and golden wingspan,
studying each rabbit track.

High above America
and watercolour Scottish hills,
in such heights you don't need engines,
boarding pass or sickness pills.

Tell me what it's like to glide
and watch the steps of little men,
skim the cliffs of Colorado,
cast a shadow down a glen.

One day there'll be cloudless vision,
one day there'll be liberty,
one day I'll be truly airborne,
when the eagle flies with me.

And
around
us...

How do you fuss an octopus?

How do you fuss an octopus?
Make it count to nine.
How do you fold an ostrich?
How many is 'a swine' –

is it singular or plural?
Do hyenas ever cry?
How long ago did starfish
fall from the ocean sky?

How do you cook a cuckoo?
When should you comb a hare?
Is the reason they're magnetic
why they're called a 'polar' bear?

And has the money spider
ever been in debt?
So does a wobbly jelly fish
take much time to set?

Is the skylark always playing
jokes above your head?
Is it possible to really tell
when a flea has fled?

Has the crouching cricket
ever played at Lords?
And watch out if that long-nosed fish
ever crosses swords.

Does a praying mantis
need to go to church?
When fishing should you take a cage
if you're catching perch?

Who stood on the flatfish?
That was really cruel.
All these questions in my head
as I walk home from school.

The first and the last

The aardvark with its hard arc,
a dome-backed curve of skin.
In every dictionary,
the first beast to go in.

While on the final pages,
a cunning beast appears.
A *zorro* ('fox' in Spanish)
as a hen bursts into tears.

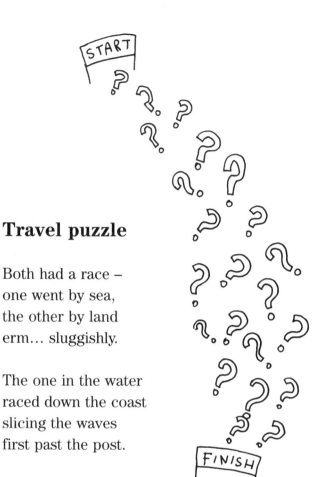

Travel puzzle

Both had a race –
one went by sea,
the other by land
erm… sluggishly.

The one in the water
raced down the coast
slicing the waves
first past the post.

His opponent left trails
that, frankly, were slime.
Can you guess what each is?
Here's a clue… their names rhyme.

Answer: A whale and a snail

The Boinngg Boinngg Bird

No one knows the Boinngg Boinngg Bird
who's never seen but always heard

it's said he bounces like a ball
and pings off clouds but best of all

is when he feeds from litter bins
which sort of act like vitamins

the rubbish which we'd never eat
is to the Boinngg Boinngg Bird a treat

for after such an awful meal
of cartons, paper, orange peel

he bounds and vaults and with one leap
he springs what's known as very steep

and it is said one straight up day
he even cleared the Milky Way

which for a bird is quite a feat
who never sings and doesn't tweet

it's sad for us the Boinngg Boinngg Bird
is never seen but always heard

now let a ruler overlap
a surface edge or table flap

and twang it with a touch so light
... for that's the Boinngg Boinngg Bird in flight

The lion who ironed his tail

The lion who ironed his tail
went on to clip his claws.
He then employed a vocal coach
to help turn off his roars.

He dyed his mane with henna
and had his teeth filed down.
Now lenses show his eyes soft blue
instead of hunting brown.

He wrote a self-help manual
on how his violence ceased,
apologized for being
this bloody-whiskered beast.

He wept his way round chat shows
but now he's being sued
by families of each ex-gazelle
that he has ever chewed.

Now no one sees him regal
and no one thinks he's strong.
He hears the jungle sniggering,
and wonders what went wrong.

Maybe icebergs...

Maybe icebergs
are frozen galleons
or Viking longboats
which lost their way
and are now
encased in drifting crystal,
in search
of some new world,
some further world.

As nearby,
on the crumbling,
Christmas cake land,
emperor penguins huddle,
hunched in ferocious winds,
a community scrum
of support and survival,
imagining lagoons
and sun terraces
without really knowing
what it is they're imagining.

Paintings that move

Across the sand or through the gorse,
leaping over Aintree's course
rides the wonder
called the Horse.

Royal duty, on parade,
gazing in a Sussex glade,
Gymkhana day
with tail of braid.

Plumed and brushed with chestnut sheen,
carries all from waif to queen,
and everyone
that's in between.

Galloping with Mustang fire.
Steaming still in Highland byre.
Filly, stallion,
Shetland, Shire.

Hear its heart and kiss its chin,
stroke the mane
and smell the skin,
neighing poems from within.

Athlete, best friend, loping grace.
Pegasus that knows its place.
Servant of
the human race.

Higher education

My school is one that trembles,
my school is one that shakes,
my school is one that's nervous,
my school is one that quakes.

My school is one that rumbles
and quivers, gargles, growls,
it sounds as if an illness
is troubling its bowels.

Inspectors never visit
and parents are too scared.
Beneath the floorboards belching
that's huge is often heard.

My school is really somewhere
that's way outside the norm...
on top of a volcano...
at least it's always warm.

Seeking work

We went out for a curry,
my hot-breathed friend and I.
He wanted my advice
as to the reason why

however much he tried,
he couldn't get a job.
He took a bite of poppadom
and then began to sob,

'I'm no good as a dragon.'
My heart was truly wrung.
He ordered vindaloo
which sadly burnt his tongue.

There is a singing chimpanzee

There is a singing chimpanzee.
The scientists asked, 'How can this be?'

And then they found a kangaroo,
with close to genius I.Q.

And next there came a dinosaur.
'But we were sure you were no more!

And is that swimming on its back
a goggled, nose-clip-wearing yak?'

By now the scientists were confused,
so baffled, flummoxed and bemused.

I wandered lonel

Then two of them began to cry
because they saw a hedgehog fly.

'We thought we were in charge of things,
it's not fair that the monkey sings,

or pocket-filled marsupials
can somehow break genetic rules.'

So at the risk of more distress
there's one small fact I should confess.

This poem, which they haven't heard,
was written by the booby bird.

And now the zoos are empty

And now the zoos are empty
the animals have left
the hay remains uneaten
the keepers are bereft.

And now the zoos are empty
a massive vacancy
the cage is full of nothing
where tiger stripes should be.

And now the zoos are empty
the wolves went in a pack
also gone the snowy owl
and squatting silver-back.*

And now the zoos are empty
reptiles, spiders, crabs
are wearing false moustaches
and hailing taxi cabs.

*a male gorilla

And now the zoos are empty
a liberated void
so many beasts are feeling
the joy of overjoyed.

And now the zoos are empty
don't tell them it was me
who put the penguins on a coach
heading for the sea.

And now the zoos are empty
the press are after me.
They call my actions 'dangerous'
and 'crass naivety'.

And now the zoos are empty
and though I've had to flee
some think I'm a heroic
eco-celebrity.

And now the zoos are empty
there's chaos everywhere
our fish shop's now 'protected'
by a gangster grizzly bear.

And now the zoos are empty
there's dung on paving stones
giraffes are being utilised
as masts for mobile phones.

And now the zoos are empty
in sweat-shops dimly lit
some ill-fed chimps are sewing
while claiming benefit.

And now the zoos are empty
we have a plague of ticks.
I've gone and started something
I don't know how to fix.

And now the zoos are empty
there's panthers breaking laws
and everyone is frightened
and everyone's indoors.

Big appetite

Inside the wardrobe
eating my coat
is a moth with a cough
with a frog in its throat.

It must have been starving –
doesn't do things by halves –
this moth who now hops, croaks
and also eats scarves.

scratched

humid night
needle bite
soon a lump
turn on light

chainsaw sound
fly flap found
enemy
gone to ground

eyes adjust
spotted – sussed
very soon
dust to dust

one mosquito
no last veto
splat on wall
farewell, finito

NOT A NICE
PICTURE
SO WE
COVERED
IT UP

King Robert the Bruce: the spider replies

(Legend tells us that a former king of Scotland, Robert the Bruce, after being defeated in a battle, ran for his life and hid in a cave. There he watched a spider make repeated attempts to build a web. At last the spider succeeded, which encouraged the king to press on and regain his crown.)

For a king he was really depressing,
he mumbled and muttered and moaned.
He was miserable, mournful and mopey
and if spiders could groan, I'd have groaned.

I said, 'Look, Jock,' but he didn't answer,
he didn't speak 'Spider', you see,
but one thing did catch his attention –
my woven web's intricacy.

He studied my efforts for hours.
I was having a terrible day
on account of him staring right at me,
'Get lost, King,' I said, 'go away.'

He put me right off but he didn't budge,
for where do kings go when they're down?
I had my patterns and pictures to plan,
he'd lost his meaning… and crown.

Yet somehow I think I inspired him,
he went on to greatness and gold.
I stayed behind unrewarded
in the dark and the damp and the cold.

And many remember his courage,
he's a high point on history's graph.
As for me I was just a mere spider,
like the one you might find in your bath.

For we're not regarded as regal
with castles and paintings to spare.
We're meagre and measly and minor…
… who hang works of art in mid-air.

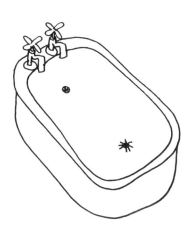

Scent of love

There is a niff
there is a stink
to send you retching
to the sink.

There is a pong
there is a reek
that's guaranteed
to leave you weak.

There is a whiff
there is a hum
that grips the throat
and turns you numb.

There is a stench
a foul aroma
that may well put
you in a coma.

No agent
will expel this odour
not lemon fresh
nor caustic soda.

The strange thing is
to lady skunks
this sick-inducing
chap's a hunk.

They think he's wicked,
drop-dead fave,
who love his gorgeous
aftershave!

The pelican

The pelican
the peli can't
the peli should
the peli shan't.

The peli did
the peli don't
the peli will
the peli won't.

The peli may
the peli might
the peli takes
a peli flight.

The peli dives –
a peli fill
of fishes
in its peli bill.

Be careful of the porcupine

Be careful of the porcupine
a rodent archer by design
a bowman with a bull's-eye quill
an armoury that moves at will.

Be wary of the porcupine
a dangerous quiver for a spine
do not approach or cause him to
direct his weapons straight at you.

Be kindly to the porcupine
his back's so sharp, he can't recline
do not go close and make him tense
he only fires in self defence.

Incident at Crufts

There is chaos at the dog show
there's a riot in the ring
as the winner proudly hobbles round
led by a piece of string

while his owner sells Big Issue
the judges are struck dumb
and a pogo-ing chihuahua
has bit one on the bum

a poodle's giving interviews
in rather frenzied French
and a tearful bloodhound's so upset
he's made an awful stench

a pekinese has fainted
and the corgi's not amused
while true to form a labrador
is muddled and confused

meanwhile the winner's showing off
he curtsies, grins and begs
his owner calls him 'Isle of Man' –
he's only got three legs

but the crowd are right behind him
there's spontaneous applause
he's now doing walking handstands
on his two front paws

and Isle of Man's not finished yet
he's relishing his win
the crowd are up and dancing
as he plays the violin

a miracle has happened
so let us all take heed;
a mongrel with three legs
can become 'the best of breed'.

The chunky monkey

The chunky monkey's on a diet
he works out and he runs
he's bought himself a treadmill
stopped eating cakes and buns

he's toning up and lycra light
so chips have had to go
and chocolate-covered anything
is certainly a 'no'

but sometimes when he's lifting weights
he has this sweet-toothed pain
and wonders if this giving up
really will sustain

him, so he's kept this book of puddings
each one with a photograph
he's cut out toffee crumble –
it's now pinned above his bath

The long-gone swan

Beside the Thames at Henley
a figure stands forlorn.
What once were snowdrift feathers
are pale and travel worn.

He stares out at the water,
as butterflies roam past,
remembering the summers
he thought would always last.

He's been away, in mourning,
on a distant estuary,
he gazes to the empty bank
where she used to be.

It seems so long to heaven,
and such an aching weight.
The long-gone swan is back again
still looking for his mate.

White-faced duck – vocal artist

(At the Wetland Centre, South West London, you can hear the white-faced duck 'whistle' every afternoon.)

The cheetah wins gold medals
for its blurring, whirring speed
and every time an otter hunts
sleek grace is guaranteed.

The twelve-point stag is regal,
the laird of lochs and thistles,
but the white-faced duck isn't fast or grand,
the white-faced duck just whistles.

He whistles bits of Mozart
and often Eminem,
when in the mood for opera
he whistles La Bohème.

He whistles blues refrains like
'Buddy, Can You Spare a Dime?'
Then whistles 'Now be Thankful',
at every feeding time.

Travel tip

Llamas wear woolly pyjamas
Grizzlies, an ankle length fur.
Neither found in the Bahamas
where, not much is best 'what to wear'.

Family gathering

I've come to the conclusion
that my mother is a toad.
She tells me to go 'hop it'.
Is that aerobic code?

My father's quite unusual,
not of the human race.
He is cosmic effluence;
i.e. a 'waste of space'.

My brother's rarely present.
I wrote down in my journal
That he's 'a fly-by-night' –
an insect that's nocturnal.

We're sitting here at dinner,
but only I can see
a toad, some rubbish and a fly,
not bothering with me.

Giant Panda's giant thoughts

*(The Giant Panda is a mainly solitary animal
although they come together for mating purposes.
At the time of writing it is estimated there are just
over one thousand of them left alive on earth.)*

I'm full of roots and crocuses
young and old bamboo,
mushrooms, gentians, not much else
but how my bottom grew.

I eat the same as yesterday
and the day before.
About tomorrow's menu,
I'm absolutely sure.

I roam the slopes of China
beneath oriental stars.
I'm also in captivity,
a quiet life behind bars.

I live alone and think a lot,
my favourite question's 'Why?'
I'm a hermit dressed in harlequin
quizzing every sky.

My eyesight's not too brilliant
but I can feel the sun,
and the impact and the greed
of the poacher's gun.

Why do you let the priceless,
the precious and the rare
then end up as a fireside rug
in some collector's lair?

In isolated forest
or San Diego zoo,
I'm not sure what I'm looking at
when I look at you.

Circus creature

High up in the bell tower
his sort of penthouse flat
he hangs from a trapeze
the so-called acro-bat

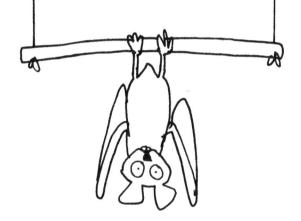

*(Note to reader – please applaud loudly
and quickly turn to next poem.)*

Deborah the zebra

Deborah the zebra
was watched by a scout –
scored a beaut,
left the goalie unsighted.

And it's no big surprise
that because of her kit
she now plays
for Newcastle United.

Holiday snaps

I've sailed from the Seychelles
to Sierra Leone
rounding the Cape of Good Hope
on my own.

I've breached with the blue whale
off Monterey.
I've sunbathed and paddled
in Montego Bay.

I've experienced storms
that lash the Azores,
and the deep, frozen imprint
of a polar bear's paws.

I've visited Margate,
there was nothing much there,
so I aimed for Morocco
via Finisterre.

Have you been to Chile,
Peru, Vietnam,
or watched the sun set
over Azerbaijan?

Have you felt the point
of a tiger shark's teeth,
or counted the coral
on the Barrier Reef?

Namibia, Mexico, Greece,
Mauritania.
Sri Lanka, Waikiki, Australia,
Albania.

This atlas of memories,
my permanent view,
the ceaseless excursions
I daily renew.

The endless, the greenness,
the blueness of me.
The vagabond voyage
of being the sea.

Emily prays to elephants

I know you're out there somewhere
making broad cloud shapes in the dark.
I know you're out there
eating good things and
trumpeting at lionesses
as they sneak towards your bare babies
with their bad, padding plans.

That's when I change channels
and watch the adverts,
it's a way of vanishing
because there's nothing I can do.

You are so big in my heart,
so perhaps we could make a pact
and I will cry with you.

What a space you must have to live in.
I see you drifting towards
warm waterholes in the buzzing heat.

I have never bathed in mud
but sometimes when my sister gets out of
    the bath
I imagine I am with you
as we lie half-submerged
in the chocolate water
listening to a flapping host of flamingos
    taking off,
a pink paradise that's always travelling…

It is all rather cramped here.
Squeezed streets with sirens
and ice cream tunes,
while you're out there
not knowing about me being here.

You glowing grey in the blazing haze;
me in the damp dusk
being driven to a swimming lesson
where I will float and pretend
that I am with you...

The elephants' reply

Thank you for your prayer, Emily.
Your singing heart arrived
in the late afternoon
between feeding
and the dipping, slipping sun.

We heard your every word,
each one carrying other thoughts
which you haven't, as yet,
said out loud.

Your awareness of our sufferings
moved us, Emily,
as we remembered
those of us
now standing on their hind legs in circuses.
And then after each performance
being locked away,
heads swaying from side to side in sorrow.

Strange that,
an elephant being made to remember,
not that we could really forget.

But one day, Emily,
because it is written somewhere
in the legends within us,
we will stamp on
every whip
and charge at chains and padlocks.
It will be the time
for the ending of such things,
they have held us all too long.

That will be a day, Emily,
when we will carry
the innocent and fragile,
and you will backstroke
through the clouds;
and then elsewhere,
but not far off,
we will be receiving
our tusks of gold.

So for now, Emily,
we think of you
in the small streets
and in the shallow end,
while we protect our babies
with all our senses
and wish you safety in your siren-streets.

We can never forget you, Emily.
Elephants never forget.

How's that done, then?

Across a still St Mary's Loch,
a crane-fly steps. Who taught her?
Both circus trick and miracle,
to walk on stilts on water.

Scuttling dreams

I'd so like to fly
but instead I just creep
I'd so like to study
the mountains asleep

I'd so like to be
at the core of a star
I'd so like a massage
whatever they are

I'd so like an orchard
baubled with peaches
I'd so like a quiet life
without all the screeches...

... but I'm in the jungle
surrounded by sound –
a lacquer black scorpion
stuck on the ground.

I give you – the sloth

In forests deeper than a cave
with heat approaching micro wave –
a creature, whose idea of fun
is dozing in the morning sun,

droops from branches, though asleep,
quite motionless without a peep.
A breathing drape of lethargy
and terrified of you and me.

An animal with little flair
who spends his days just hanging there,
a mammal mobile lacking breeze,
a decoration for the trees.

If he made an aerobics tape
you'd see him as a hammock shape,
suspended, still and quite serene,
his fur furred up with fungal green.

So let us now salute the sloth
who's just too tired to be a both.
'To move' for him's a pointless verb.
His aim in life? – 'Do Not Disturb'.

Palette life

(The chameleon can dramatically change the shading of its body in order to blend in with its surroundings.)

On a carpet of leaves
you can't see that I'm there.
I can even do toupees,
black, brown or fair.

Sometimes I'm a painting
from head down to shin,
a dazzling sunflower,
Van Gogh as my skin.

I'm fire engine red
and indigo blue.
I'm a multi of colours,
I could even do you.

My swivel eyes study
and then I begin.
I stand next to macaws
which does their heads in.

I once met a rainbow
and copied each hue.
Now luminous stripes
are quite easy to do.

I've yet to try clouds
or a pelican's wings.
And one day I'd love
to attempt Saturn's rings.

But there's one awkward challenge
that makes my brain wilt.
I'm in such a muddle
as I cling to this kilt.

Have you spotted me yet?

Evening meal

A rat who adores ratatouille
is likely to order it gooey
as opposed to quite raw
which takes ages to gnaw
and tastes blecch!!!! 'cos it's terribly chewy

Can't think where I put it...

Useful thing
a pouch
just ask the kangaroo
keeps her babies there
a crèche
with a bounding view.

But somehow
the koala's
handy little sack
is nowhere near its tummy
but somewhere
round the back.

We're going out to count the birds

We're going out to count the birds,
the butterflies and bugs,
the parakeets and furry bees
and, if there's time, the slugs.

We're going out to watch the swans,
the moorhens and the coots,
then with our calculator
we'll add up all the newts.

We're going out to stare at frogs
and mallards as they preen,
to wake the snoozing heron
as we bash our tambourine.

And you will play your xylophone,
then as it's getting dark
we'll leave the daily carnival
that is our public park.

We'll head off home for burgers
and chips the shape of trees
with onion rings that quietly sing
and strawberry-flavoured peas.

Lonely heart

Marmoset, fragile pet,
nervy, rarely still,
hates alone, far from home,
pining for Brazil.

It could happen...

A bat with a kaleidoscope,
a walrus in a tree,
a friendless, tuneless gargoyle
winning Fame Academy.

Everything is possible
and anything could be.
The falcon sailing with the vole
towards the risen sea.

Creation rave

You can hear the swamps and forests
and oceans' sonic tunes.
You can listen to the latest hits
downloaded by baboons.

For from every web and waterhole
to every bear-lined cave
ceaseless beasts are making peace
at a monster, mammoth rave.

The jungle's jazzed and jumping
the seas buzz with the beat.
Hip hop ducks go flip flop
on account of their webbed feet.

Rhinoceros glow phosphorous
on the strobe-lit floor
and a pig with tusks
is tame with love – no longer a wild boar.

High-fiving techno geckos
mix the licks and scratch the decks
blissed-out giraffes stay cool
while chimps race up and down their necks.

In the milling, spilling chill-out room
the vibes are groovy blue
– that's not some stuffed toys snoring
but a crashed koala crew.

There are ants formation dancing
and jiving caribou
spin on their hooves and learn new moves
from a hip, break-dancing shrew.

And every creature's partying
and every species bops
and the earth's a bass line, boom box
at the rave that never stops…
that never stops…
that never stops…

And below us

The dolphin who found his smile

There once was a dolphin,
in fact there still is,
who grins as he swims
and at swims he's the biz.

He fizzes the ocean with
dashes and dips
then high jumps the waves
with giggling flips.

He snorkels, he chuckles,
he stands up, he clicks,
and juggling shells
is just one of his tricks.

The sea is his playground
where he keeps all his toys
like seaweed and moonlight
and light-flashing buoys.

He curls and he whirls
and he swirls and he japes.
He's a prize and a present
of interesting shapes.

A starfish once asked him,
and so did a seal,
where his happiness came from
and what made it so real?

'Have I never told you,'
said the dolphin with glee,
'how jumping joy happiness
came back to me?

'One day while out dreaming
I thought I misplaced
this crescent moon smile
that brightens my face.

'So I searched and I worried,
I was drowning in fear
but then I woke up
and my smile was still here!'

Though sleep had confused him,
it just wasn't so
that his smile in the darkness
had decided to go.

Like the mountain in mist
or the thrush with its song,
the smile and the dolphin
are meant to belong.

Shock tactics

The torpedo ray
the torpedo ray
electrical sniper
zapping its prey
on the sea bed
avoiding display
the 1000-watt shock
of the torpedo ray.

The torpedo ray
the torpedo ray
sly generator
you can't keep at bay
a depth charge assassin
ready to slay
the hydro attack
of the torpedo ray.

The torpedo ray
the torpedo ray
whatever you are
you'll have no say
sharks won't go near
whales keep away
from the deadly discharge
of the torpedo ray.

Marine jelly

Amphipod,
transparent bod,
a gleaming glass disguise.
A roaming
see-through light bulb,
jelly bean-like eyes.

Diamond clear,
deep chandelier.
slowly somersaults.
A rare,
revolving X-ray
in the ocean's vaults.

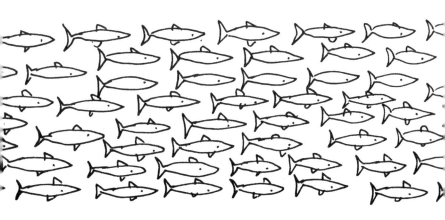

Underwater incubator

Slight and swift
the same fish
but many times.

Blue-green patterns
on its back.
Like a shuffled rainbow
or shaded, sea pearls
or silk swimming –
a kimono at thirty miles an hour.

And off the south-west coast of Ireland
every teeming spring
each female mackerel
lays half a million eggs

half a million eggs

half a million eggs

half a million eggs.

The same fish

half a million times
each.

The sea horse is a fish

The sea horse is a fish
with a small snout
the sea horse is not a pig

the sea horse uses its snout
to suck in its food
the sea horse is not a vacuum cleaner

the sea horse possesses
independently moving eyes
the sea horse is not a chameleon

the sea horse wears
a crown on its head
every crown is different
the sea horse is not a king or queen

the sea horse is
brilliant at disguise
and is very difficult to find
the sea horse is not in the SAS

the sea horse dances
with its partner every morning
the sea horse has its own music

the sea horse is monogamous
(the sea horse suggests
you look that word up)

the sea horse often swims
with its partner
their tails entwined
the sea horse is quite romantic

the sea horse which
gives birth to baby sea horses
is not the female but the male
the sea horse does things completely differently

the sea horse can
take several days to give birth
during this time it continues to dance
the sea horse is not like us

the sea horse has
no scales on its body
the sea horse is a fish

What a pet

Why can't you be like others
with an ordinary pet?
It really isn't funny
to completely eat the vet.

Why can't you keep a hamster,
a budgie or a cat?
A snake I could accept,
fat with a swallowed rat.

Why can't you just be normal?
I must have gone quite soft,
to build and fill a swimming pool
above us in the loft.

The joists are really straining
while the ceiling's getting low,
plus, the vet's bag now is evidence.
That shark has got to go!